THAT'S A JOB?

I like the OUTDOORS

... what jobs are there?

by Carron Brown

Illustrated by Roberto Blefari

Kane Miller
A DIVISION OF EDC PUBLISHING

CONTENTS

INTRODUCTION

Qualities and skills for working in the outdoors

There are lots of jobs that involve working outdoors, some of which you may not even know existed.

Do you love the great outdoors? Is nature important to you? If so, you can turn this passion into a career!

From jobs in science, conservation, and construction, to farming and teaching, there are many opportunities for people who want to work outside.

Each job needs different people with different skills: land surveyors must be good with numbers and detail; geologists and marine biologists need strong science qualifications; travel writers must have great writing skills, while ski instructors might need patience when teaching nervous students.

But there are some qualities that everyone who works outdoors should have: a can-do attitude, a sense of adventure, and, most importantly, a respect for nature. From park rangers to ecologists—taking care of the environment is very important.

Many jobs require teamwork and physical fitness. For instance, lifeguards have to trust and depend on each other, and line workers need to be strong climbers. Sometimes you might need to be quite brave, too—for example, wildland firefighters often face danger to save and protect others.

Whatever the job, you'll always need to be ready for any weather and to remember to be safe. The outdoors can bring unexpected challenges so safety for yourself, for others, and for nature always comes first.

If all this sounds like you, then you're the right type of person to work in the outdoors!

This book looks at 25 different jobs that involve working outdoors, giving you a sneak peek into a typical day in the life of each worker. You'll learn the important stuff, like what it takes to get the job, and what duties and tasks are involved, and you'll discover the fun stuff too, such as the worst part of a surf instructor's job ...

HINT: It involves sand and wetsuits!

When you've read about all the different jobs in the book, turn to page 44 to find out which jobs might suit you, or page 46 to discover even more jobs!

MARINE BIOLOGIST

When I was younger, I watched a TV series about marine (ocean) life, and I've been fascinated ever since. I worked hard in science and math at school and went to college to study marine science. Now I'm working on a research project in the icy Southern Ocean around Antarctica.

1

Today, I wake up in my cabin to the sounds of waves. I'm on a research ship studying plastic particles (tiny pieces of plastic) on the ocean surface. There are now billions of these particles floating around our oceans, and I am here to investigate how they are affecting marine life.

2

After breakfast, my first task is to catch some plastic particles from the ocean surface. I head out on deck with my assistant. It's very cold so we wrap up warm, and we put on our hard hats and life jackets for safety.

When I'm not on a research trip, I'm in a laboratory back home analyzing data, writing reports, and reading other marine biologists' work. I'm always learning. Marine biologists can specialize in all kinds of ocean life, from huge whales to tiny sea creatures.

3

We get the equipment ready. The ship's crew helps us attach a special net to the back of the boat. We throw the net down and it drags behind the boat, catching the particles.

VOYAGES OF DISCOVERY

Research ships can carry up to 100 people. As well as the crew, there are scientists who study the oceans, marine life, or the environment, such as oceanographers, marine biologists, and ecologists. They all spend weeks out at sea, discovering more about our fascinating oceans.

4

We take what we've collected to the ship's laboratory and look at the particles under a microscope—they are so tiny that we can't see them without one. We're looking for any tiny creatures that may live on the particles, to see if they could be harmful to the environment.

5

Once we've finished, we break for lunch. The sea is a bit rough today, so we have to hold on to our plates!

7

Once the orcas have swum away, we collect more plastic samples. I finish the day writing notes for my report. I work long hours to make the most of the research trip.

6

After lunch, we go back on deck to collect more plastic. But there's a problem: we can't drop the net because a pod of orcas is swimming close by and we don't want to disturb them. I don't mind the wait though—I love watching these amazing creatures.

8

It's 7:30 p.m. and time for dinner with the other scientists on the ship. I sit next to a glaciologist who's studying how fast the ice is melting in Antarctica. I love hearing about what the other scientists are doing. But I think I've got the best job.

MY JOB: BEST AND WORST PARTS

BEST: Exploring the marine world is incredible— and there is still so much more to learn.

WORST: Seasickness! The winds and waves can be wild, but you get used to it.

TRAVEL WRITER

Life as a travel writer is full of adventure. I often wake up in a different place several days in a row! After completing my journalism degree, I traveled around the world, blogging my experiences. I loved it so much that I now make a living from writing and selling my articles to magazines and websites.

I've traveled to over 80 countries across all seven continents. I've seen amazing sights, from hot-air balloon festivals to the world's biggest waterfalls.

1

I've just arrived in New Delhi, India's capital city. An online magazine for disabled travelers has asked me to write an article about wheelchair-friendly things to do in New Delhi. I can't wait to get started!

2

I began researching on the flight here, but when I arrive at my hotel, I finish planning some interesting things to do around New Delhi. I browse some travel blogs and local people's social media posts about the city.

MY JOB: BEST AND WORST PARTS

BEST: I love the adventure. I also enjoy helping other wheelchair users get the best out of their traveling experiences.

WORST: Jet lag! I lose a lot of sleep while traveling. And waiting in line for attractions can be boring, too.

3

Next, I meet a tour guide who's going to show me the sights. My guide knows all the places that are easy to get around, such as those with ramps or without stairs.

4

As we drive through the busy streets, I make notes and take photos. On some trips, a travel photographer will accompany me, but often I take the pictures as well as write the words.

5

We're soon at the Red Fort, one of New Delhi's most visited historic buildings. It's over 400 years old and it gets its name from its beautiful red sandstone walls. What a feast for the eyes! There are gardens, palaces, and canals, and plenty of ramps so I have no problems getting around.

6

Next, we head to one of the city's bazaars, a market selling clothes, souvenirs, and street food such as samosas and chai (spiced, milky tea). It's a fantastic place! I take lots of photos of the people and colorful stalls. I'll send them to the editor of the article, who will choose which pictures to use.

7

After trying many tasty treats and taking lots of notes and pictures, it's time to return to the hotel. I post some photos on my website and social media profiles. It's important for me to do this as it helps show my work and can lead to more assignments.

8

Before bed, I start writing the article about today's tour while it's still fresh in my mind. I'll work on it again tomorrow after I've spent another day exploring the fascinating sights of New Delhi!

GEOLOGIST

I enjoyed science at school, and loved collecting interesting rocks—my bedroom was full of them! In college, I studied geoscience and I learned all about the formation of our amazing planet. After my studies, I worked as an intern, and now I work for a construction company. I test land to see if it can be built on. There are always problems to solve and new discoveries to make.

Geologists aren't just rock experts. They can specialize in other areas, such as volcanoes (a volcanologist), underground water (a hydrogeologist), or climate change (an environmental geologist).

1

At 8:00 a.m., I arrive on site. The construction company is planning to build several houses, so I'm here to check that the ground is suitable. I meet the drilling team, who will drill into the earth to collect a sample of rock for me to study. It's the first of many samples I will be testing over the next weeks.

2

The drillers use a machine called a rig to drill a long, hollow tube into the ground. The tube pulls out a length of rock, which we place in a tray. I record where the rock was drilled from, and how deep we drilled. It's amazing to think that parts of this rock are millions of years old.

3

In the afternoon, I drive to the lab and examine the sample under a powerful microscope, which lets me see all the minerals (solid, natural substances) the rock is made of. I record the data and add it to the 3-D digital map of the site I've been working on. The architect will use this map to see where the houses can be built, so it has to be accurate.

4

I finish the day writing up my findings. So far it looks as though the ground is suitable. But it's too early to call; tomorrow I'll be back on site— who knows what I might discover.

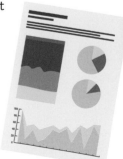

MY JOB: BEST AND WORST PARTS

BEST: I love the mix of field and lab work.

WORST: The work can be very wet and muddy, and there can be spiders and bugs to avoid, too!

PALEONTOLOGIST

My job is to dig for fossils, to find out about creatures that lived millions of years ago. I found my first fossil on the beach when I was eight years old, and I've been hooked ever since. It took years of learning science at school, geology in college, and more specialist study to get my job, and it's all been worth it.

1

Today I'm on a research trip in the desert, looking for dinosaur remains, such as bones, tracks, or even poop! I arrive on site with other paleontologists, who have been sent by museums and colleges from around the world to help with the research. We'll be outdoors all day—luckily, it's dry and sunny.

I work for a natural history museum, where I look after the exhibits and talk to visitors about them. I also go on trips to dig for fossils, in the hope I'll learn more about creatures from the past.

2

By looking at special geological maps, we already know the age of the rock on this site. This means fossils from the same time period might also be here. We spot an area where the rock has worn away—and look, fossils!

3

The fossils look like the remains of dinosaur bones. We spend the whole day carefully beginning to dig them out. We wrap each one in a plaster cast to keep it safe, like the cast around a broken arm.

MY JOB: BEST AND WORST PARTS

BEST: Working with, and learning from, specialists around the world.

WORST: It can take weeks to unearth just one fossil, so you need a lot of patience!

4

After hours of digging, we make sure the site is sheltered and pack up our findings to take back to the lab. A fossil preparator will piece together the bones so we can get a better idea of what kind of dinosaur we have unearthed. It's very exciting. I can't wait to continue the work tomorrow.

LANDSCAPE GARDENER

My work as a landscape gardener means I'm often outdoors six days a week, rain or shine. I started out as an apprentice for another company and now I run my own business. I don't just plant flowers and pull up weeds: I'm also an expert at building paths and fences, laying out patios, and even painting and decorating. It's the kind of job that needs creativity and lots of energy.

Landscape gardeners work in all kinds of outdoor spaces, from private gardens and parks to hospital gardens.

1

At 7:30 a.m., my team and I arrive at a local hospital. We have been hired to create a beautiful new outdoor space that staff, patients, and visitors can enjoy. The plans include a path for people to stroll on, flower beds, and benches to sit and relax on.

2

After a quick team meeting, we get started building the new path. It will need to be flat, and wide enough for wheelchairs. I measure and mark out the path using string and poles. Good math skills are handy in this job—you need to get the measurements right.

3

I leave half of my team to continue digging the path, while the rest of us start planting the flower beds. We work hard, only stopping for a quick lunch before we're back to work. It's amazing to see the progress. The flowers are already attracting butterflies— the first to enjoy our work.

MY JOB: BEST AND WORST PARTS

BEST: Seeing people enjoy a finished garden is very rewarding.

WORST: I'm often at the mercy of the weather. If it's pouring with rain or too dark, I can't work.

4

At 5:00 p.m., we pack up our tools, and make sure the site is tidy and safe before calling it a day. Tomorrow's sure to be just as busy!

PLANT NURSERY MANAGER

Working as a plant nursery manager is nonstop—there's always a lot to do! I love it because I can use my knowledge of horticulture (the science of growing garden plants) to care for the plants, advise customers on which plants to buy, and help make the nursery successful.

To become a plant nursery manager, you often need to get a horticulture degree or professional training in nursery management. Hands-on experience working in nurseries is also important.

1

Since there's always plenty to do, I usually get to work before the nursery opens. Today, for example, I take a delivery of young trees. It's my job to choose and order plants from suppliers and organize deliveries like this one. The nursery assistants help me unload the trees and check them for any damage.

2

Next, we make sure the store displays are tidy and all the plants are watered and healthy, with no signs of disease or bugs. We open the doors at 9:00 a.m. and the customers soon arrive. It's a busy morning and I love helping people find what they need. One customer is looking for flowers to plant in her garden. I show her some climbing yellow roses, which she agrees would be perfect.

3

We sometimes run events for our customers, and this afternoon there's a workshop, where customers learn how to plant hanging baskets. We get the baskets, soil, and plants ready. During the workshop, I take photos for the nursery website. Everyone's having fun!

MY JOB: BEST AND WORST PARTS

BEST: Customers sometimes show me pictures of their beautiful gardens filled with plants they've bought here.

WORST: I don't like seeing plants get sick, and do my best to get rid of the bad bugs that damage them. Luckily, not all bugs are bad. Some good bugs even eat the bad bugs!

4

Soon it's the end of the day. Before I leave, I check the weather forecast for tonight. It looks like we're in for some strong winds. I make sure all the plants are safely sheltered so they don't blow over.

13

WILDLIFE OFFICER

It's my job to protect the animals and plant life here on the wildlife refuge. I make sure visitors follow the fishing and hunting laws, and I also teach them about the refuge. I had to do specialist training to get my job. I learned about the law, and about wildlife, and I also had to do physical training to show that I was fit enough.

1

Today I start the morning helping a group of biologists. They have been caring for some otters and will be releasing them to live in the refuge. They want to film their behavior when they're back in the wild and study it. Assisting with conservation projects like this one is one of the best parts of my job. I help them set up the cameras before getting on with my morning.

In my job, I work with lots of different people, including scientists, young people, and other members of the public. I love helping people protect the natural world around us.

2

Next, I patrol the refuge on foot. I check that everything is in order and make sure that fences and gates haven't been damaged or broken. Wildlife officers tend to work alone, and refuges can be very big, so I always carry a compass and GPS device in case I get lost.

3

I've almost finished my patrol when I spot some lost mountain bikers riding off the bike trail. I direct them back to the trail and wave goodbye as they zoom off. The bikes damage plants if they aren't on the trail, and the plants provide important food for the animals.

MY JOB: BEST AND WORST PARTS

BEST: The outdoors is my office, and I love it!

WORST: I'm on call 24 hours a day, so I often get called in at night and on weekends.

4

In the afternoon, I do a boat patrol along the river. I'm looking for anyone fishing or hunting illegally, or breaking any other laws. I'm also watching for wild animals, in case I need to alert refuge visitors and move them away for their safety.

5

I soon spot some anglers (people fishing) and make my way over to them. We've had trouble recently with people fishing without permits, so today I'm checking every angler I see. I smile and politely ask to see their permits. Bravery is a good trait to have for this job, as sometimes people can be angry if they're caught breaking the rules. Luckily, these anglers are friendly and have the right permits.

6

Next, I head to the visitor center. Part of my job involves educating others about the refuge, and today I'm teaching a group of children all about the wildlife here. I explain that having laws and rules to protect the animals and resources on the refuge means we can all continue to enjoy them.

7

After the teaching session, I settle down with some paperwork. I recently caught some criminals poaching (illegally hunting) deer from the refuge. I'm writing a report that will be used in court as evidence that will hopefully bring them to justice.

8

I'm just about ready to go home when I hear a "ping" and look at my phone to see a photo from one of the biologists I met earlier—it shows the otter family on the move! Seeing this photo is a wonderful end to my day.

FORESTER

I love forests. There's always something new to see, be it animals, plants, or trees. My job as a forester means I look after forest trees and wildlife. I plan which trees can be cut down, where to plant new trees, and I make sure that people can visit and enjoy the forest. I studied forest management in college and built up work experience before I got my job.

You have to be fit in my job. I'm outside most of the day, hiking all over the forest. Being calm is also important, since I sometimes have to face risky situations such as forest fires, storms, or wild animals.

1

My day starts in the office, reviewing our forest management plan. This is a document full of information on our forest, including its size, and details on the creatures that live here. Updating the plan is a big part of my job.

2

Next, I head outside with one of the forestry technicians. We are due to cut some trees down, and it's up to me to select which ones. We start out by measuring trunks; this tells us how much wood each tree has. Once we select a tree to be cut, we mark its trunk.

3

We look for trees that might be used by animals, since we don't want to cut these down. Nests in branches mean that birds could return again, and holes in trees can be homes for squirrels.

MY JOB: BEST AND WORST PARTS

BEST: I love to be organized and plan ahead, which is great since it's a huge part of my job.

WORST: Forest fires can be very devastating.

4

In the afternoon, I take a look at a new trail we're making, and I'm delighted with the progress. Soon, visitors will be able to use the trail to see new parts of the forest they couldn't get to before.

5

I finish the day back in the office, updating the forest management plan. Soon it's home time—I don't have far to go—I love the forest so much that I chose a home right on the edge of it!

WILDLAND FIREFIGHTER

I was always athletic at school, and I wanted a job that was active and that helped people. Wildland firefighting checked all the right boxes, so I joined the fire service. I had to do special training to learn about fire science and first aid. I also did lots of fitness training, including running with a heavy backpack! Being a firefighter is tough, but I love it.

1

It's 6:45 a.m. when I arrive at the fire station today, just in time for the morning briefing. It's summer, and the local forests and woodlands are very dry, so we're on high alert for possible fires. After the briefing, I spend the morning checking some of our equipment, making sure it's ready if we need it.

2

After lunch, a call comes through from the pilot of a fire-spotting helicopter. It's the pilot's job to look for wildfires from the air, and she has seen a small one nearby, likely caused by a campfire. We set off with our equipment into the forest.

Firefighters work together as a team to keep people safe. But we don't just put out fires. Some deal with other emergencies, such as car accidents or collapsed buildings. We also teach people fire safety and how to prevent fires from starting.

3

We start digging a fire line all the way around the fire to stop it from spreading. This involves cutting back plants to just the bare soil so that when the fire reaches the line there is nothing to burn.

MY JOB: BEST AND WORST PARTS

BEST: I love being able to save people's lives and homes by stopping wildfires.

WORST: It's frustrating when people cause fires by not following the safety rules.

4

Now it's time for water. We guide the hoses from a huge water tank to the fire and water gushes onto the flames. Meanwhile, a helicopter releases water from above. After hours of physical, dusty work, the fire is starting to die down, at last.

5

When we're sure that the fire has stopped, we pack up and head back to the station. I'm exhausted, but happy it's been a successful day's work!

17

CAMPSITE MANAGER

Growing up, my family went camping every summer, and that's what got me interested in working on a campsite. I thought it would be fun—and I was right! I started as an assistant and became a manager after learning all the skills needed to run a campsite and look after staff and visitors. There's a lot going on all the time, so it's lucky I love to be busy.

In my job, you have to be on call all day—one minute I'm fixing a sign, the next I'm suggesting a good hiking route.

1

Good morning! My day starts early at 7:00 a.m., like always. Most campers are asleep, but there are a few people ready to check out early, so I take care of that and wave goodbye to them. Next, I pin up the day's weather report on the bulletin board and meet the cleaner. He reports that the bathroom blocks are sparkling clean and all is well.

2

After final checkout at 11:30 a.m., I walk around the site to make sure everything's tidy and that no one has left anything. I spot a damaged fence and call a contractor to come by later today to fix it.

3

I head back to the office to check my emails and any phone messages. Campers get in touch all day long with enquiries and reservations. I log the reservations on my computer.

MY JOB: BEST AND WORST PARTS

BEST: Meeting people from all around the world and listening to their stories is really exciting.

WORST: It's sad when I find a site covered in litter. People should always place what they don't want to take home in the recycling or trash.

4

In the afternoon, new campers arrive. Our campsite assistant hands them a map and a guide to the site, and walks them to their camping spot. In the guide is a list of rules. These include being quiet at night, keeping away from animals, only lighting a fire in a special firepit, and making sure the fire is out before leaving.

GUIDE

5

One family has already pitched their tent and are ready for some fun. A big part of my job is knowing all about the surrounding area and available activities. I tell them about a lake nearby where they can swim and kayak, point out an excellent mountain bike trail, and leave them to their plans.

6

At 3:00 p.m., the contractor arrives and gets to work. The fence helps keep larger animals out of the campsite, which is safer for the campers and for curious creatures.

SORRY WE ARE
FULL

7

When all the campers have arrived, I flip the campsite sign to say "FULL." I spend the rest of the afternoon in our store, selling firewood and food, and answering campers' questions.

8

At around 7:30 p.m., the assistant and I close the office and say good night to the campers who are relaxing or cooking an evening meal. There's an emergency number if they need someone while the office is closed. Both the assistant and I live close by, so help is always near.

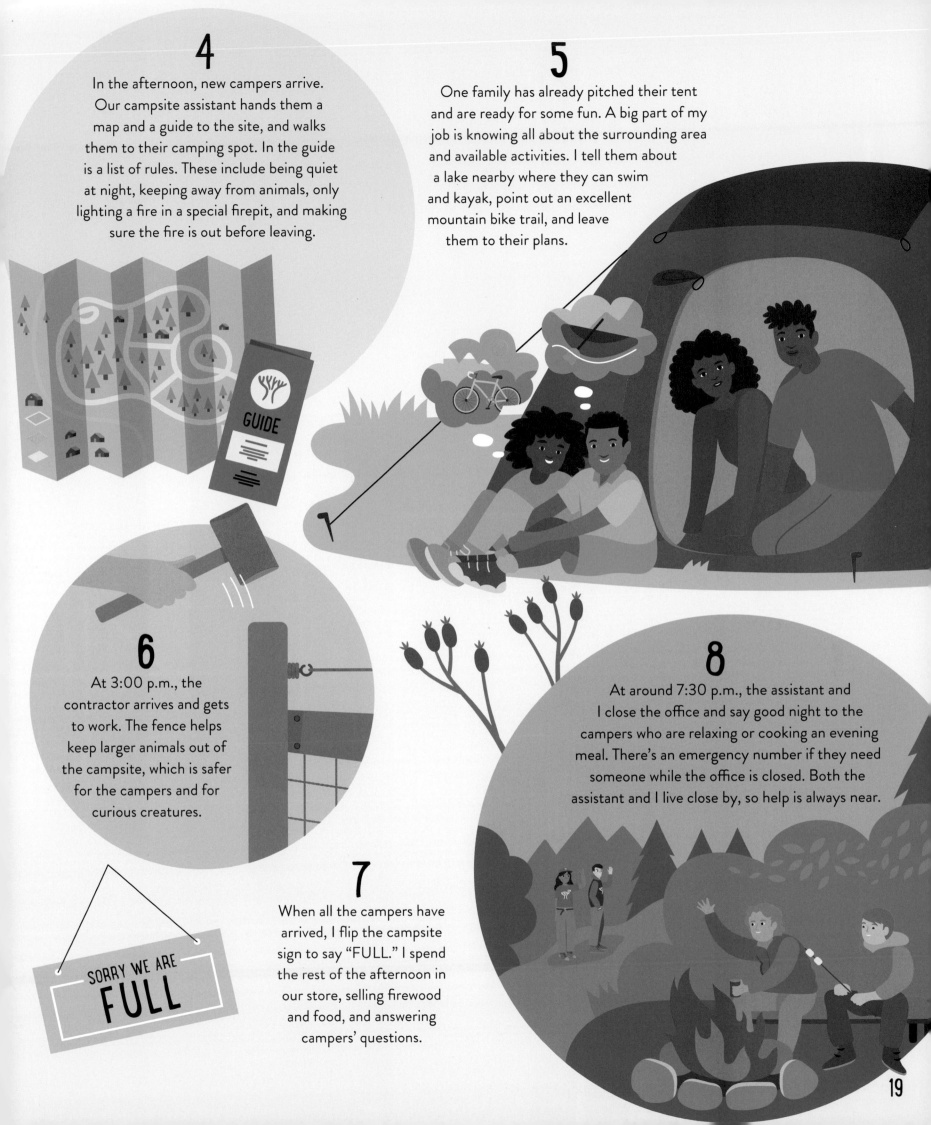

CONSTRUCTION SITE MANAGER

Helping to create magnificent buildings is my dream job. After studying construction management in college, I worked as an assistant for a construction company. I learned on the job, working my way up, and now I manage large building projects. I make sure a building is completed on time, safely, and that the clients are happy.

1

It's 7:30 a.m. and I'm in my office, checking my to-do list. With several projects on the go at once, I have to be organized. Today, I'll be visiting one of our sites where we're building a brand-new supermarket.

I work for a big company that oversees all kinds of different building projects, including skyscrapers, shopping malls, apartments, and schools. Some construction managers set up and run their own companies.

2

When I arrive at the site, I meet with the foreman. I can't be everywhere at once, so I hire foremen to work on each site and make sure everyone's doing a good job. He shows me the blueprints (plans) and tells me we're on schedule, and so far, no problems. I sure love hearing that!

3

Next, I take a look around the site. It's amazing to see how quickly it has changed. Just a few months ago this was a patch of grass! I check that the site is safe, that there are no hazards, and that the workers are following the rules, such as wearing hard hats. Health and safety is very important.

4

After a quick lunch with the team, I meet with the architect to discuss progress. Most of the structural work (the walls and roof) is finished, and now carpenters, electricians, and plumbers are hard at work on the inside of the building. It's noisy and busy.

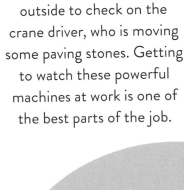

5

After the meeting, I head outside to check on the crane driver, who is moving some paving stones. Getting to watch these powerful machines at work is one of the best parts of the job.

6

Next, I catch up with the landscape gardener who has designed a plan for the parking lot outside. Along with spaces for cars, she is planning flower beds and benches to create a beautiful, welcoming space.

7

Everything is going well ... until it starts to rain! We stop all outside tasks because it's unsafe to work with heavy machinery or to be up on high scaffolds in bad weather.

8

The site closes at 5:00 p.m. and I head home. I keep my phone on, just in case there's an overnight emergency on a site, such as strong winds knocking over equipment. But hopefully I won't get any calls.

MY JOB: BEST AND WORST PARTS

BEST: Watching an owner's happy reaction to the finished building.

WORST: It can be stressful trying to get a project completed on time. And being in the office isn't much fun—I prefer to be on site where all the action is.

SKI INSTRUCTOR

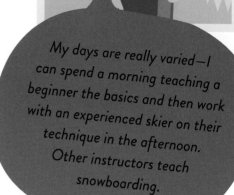

I grew up in the mountains and learned to ski at school. It didn't take long for me to be hooked, and I've skied every winter since. After I passed my ski instructor training I joined the local ski school, and now I spend my days teaching people of all ages.

My days are really varied—I can spend a morning teaching a beginner the basics and then work with an experienced skier on their technique in the afternoon. Other instructors teach snowboarding.

1

I start the day like always—taking time for breakfast! This is important since my job is physical and I need energy to get me through the morning. Today, it's oatmeal with fruit and honey. Next, I dress in my uniform and catch the bus to the ski school.

2

I arrive at 8:25 a.m., in time for the morning meeting where the instructors go through the day's schedule. Today I'm working with another instructor, and together we will be teaching a group of children. They're all beginners so we'll start out on the flattest and gentlest runs.

3

We get our gear and meet our students, who are waiting excitedly with their parents. We check that the children are dressed warmly and that their ski boots are on. The parents leave, and I start the lesson with a simple game of "copy me." The students copy my movements, starting with some stretches to get them warmed up.

4

Next, I show the students some basic ski moves, such as the snowplow, which helps to control speed and to stop. When we feel the students have the hang of it, we all take the rope tow to the top of the run.

5

We line up with me at the front and my partner at the back, and we slowly snowplow down. We make lots of wide turns instead of going straight all the way down; it's safer and slower this way. I ski backward so I can check on the students, and my partner is there to help any of them if they fall. We ski down the run several times, and soon they're all feeling confident.

6

At lunchtime, we head to the ski school and I help the children out of their wet gloves and coats. We eat in the warmth, going over the fun we've had so far.

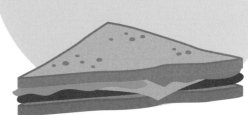

7

Heading out for the afternoon lesson, we see an emergency helicopter coming in to land. It's likely that someone has had an accident and needs to go to the hospital. Luckily there are plenty of ski patrollers at this ski resort. They are trained in first aid and look out for the health and safety of skiers on the mountain. Along with the helicopter crew, they will make sure the injured skier gets the best care.

8

We go over the basic moves again and even ski down another slightly steeper run. The time flies, and soon we're back indoors waiting for the parents. While the children talk about their skiing adventures, I write report cards to give to the parents.

MY JOB: BEST AND WORST PARTS

BEST: Before, between, and after lessons, I can ski.

WORST: I miss skiing when the season ends. And falling headfirst into freezing snow isn't much fun!

9

After waving goodbye to the children, I head to my favorite runs to do some skiing on my own before the resort closes. The season is nearly over and soon the snow will melt. But I won't be leaving—I spend my summers here too, working as a mountain guide.

ECOLOGIST

When I was young, I wanted to know the name of every animal and flower I saw. I loved biology in school, so I went on to study environmental science in college and volunteer with a conservation charity. As an ecologist, I study how plants and animals survive in their surroundings and with each other.

1

I'm working on a project to protect and encourage plant and insect life in our cities. Insects such as bees and butterflies pollinate plants, helping them to reproduce (create more plants). We humans rely on plants for our food, clothing, and other things, so protecting both plants and insects is very important.

Many plant and animal species are in danger of dying out. In my job, I look at how humans are affecting our natural world and what we can do to protect it.

2

I meet with my team of scientists at a local park. We are spending the morning counting insects that are pollinating the plants in the city. I want to find out which plants the insects are most attracted to. We can then protect those plants so the insects will keep coming back and the plants will keep growing.

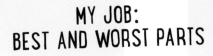

MY JOB: BEST AND WORST PARTS

BEST: My job gives me the chance to protect our natural world and help people understand why that's important.

WORST: Bee stings and bugs flying up my nose!

3

To count the insects, we measure a grassy area by putting down lines of tape called transects. Then we walk down our transects, sweeping from side to side with our nets to catch the insects.

4

I'm lucky enough to catch a beautiful blue butterfly. I gently place it in my container so I don't hurt it. I make a note of it and then carefully release it.

5

Next, we put down square frames called quadrats along each transect line. In each frame, we identify and write down the plants we find.

6

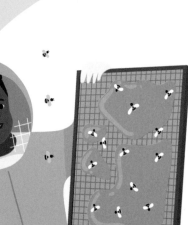

After lunch, I make my way to the park beehives. The beekeeper gives me honey from the hives, but I won't be eating it for breakfast; I'll take it to our science lab to find out which plants the bees have visited to create the honey.

CITIZEN SCIENCE

Ecologists often work with volunteers who record sightings of wildlife and plants in a local area or their garden. This is called citizen science. Look for a project, such as a winter bird watch, near you.

7

It's nearly the end of the day, so I head back to the office. I log today's research on the computer. Tomorrow, I will write a report about which plants we need to keep growing in our city so we can provide happy homes for all our bees, butterflies, and other amazing bugs.

ADVENTURE GUIDE

My job is to make sure people have a great, safe day in the outdoors. Each day is different—I'm white-water rafting one day, and the next I'm hiking into the wilderness. At school, I worked part-time at an indoor climbing wall, then I trained for climbing certificates and wilderness first aid, and then I found that there were many more outdoor activities to master.

I have to be alert all the time, since I'm responsible for the safety of each person in my group. I work for an adventure guide business, which I love because I like to be part of a team.

1

The first thing I do today is check the forecast. I'm heading to the mountains to teach a group how to climb, and I want to be prepared for the weather. The students are told to wear appropriate clothes for climbing and bring waterproof jackets—but people often forget, so I always bring sunscreen and extra waterproof gear.

2

I'm working with a trainee adventure guide today, and together we pick up the packed lunches and the gear—including ropes, gloves, helmets, harnesses, maps, and the first aid kit. We reach the parking lot 15 minutes before the group arrives. It's good to be early to go through the route together, choose the area where we should have lunch, and discuss any potentially tricky situations, such as steep paths or crossing water.

3

The gear is handed out to the group. I then introduce what we'll be doing, and how each person is responsible for taking care of nature. I ask them not to drop litter, pick flowers, or walk toward wild animals. Then we're off!

MY JOB: BEST AND WORST PARTS

BEST: Spending my days climbing cliffs and being outdoors is my idea of a good time.

WORST: Cleaning the muddy and wet gear at the end of a bad weather day.

4

It takes half an hour to reach the cliff we'll be climbing, and we chat and admire the views as we hike. We stop just before the cliff to put on our helmets—rocks can fall from the cliff so it's important we're all as protected as we can be. While the trainee guide helps the group into their gear, I head to the top of the cliff to anchor the systems that will hold the climbing ropes securely.

5

After making the final checks at the top, I head down to make doubly sure that everyone is safely in their gear. I teach two of the group how to climb at a time, with one person going up and the other person on the ground holding the rope that has a device to stop a fall. I stay on the ground to supervise and help others climb, while the trainee helps the climbers at the top.

6

I follow the last climber up to the top and it's smiles all around. We sit in the shade, eat our lunch, and take in the view. We chat about how scared people were before the climb and how they've conquered their fears.

7

Soon it's time to go down again. We teach the group how to rappel. One by one, the climbers line up and their harnesses are secured on the rappel line before they're guided down slowly. I see a moment of fear followed by a big smile as each person realizes it's safe and fun. We take photos so they can have a keepsake of their day.

8

With everyone at the bottom, we begin the walk back to the parking lot. I enjoy hearing how everyone has learned some new skills. Once back at the office, the trainee unpacks the gear, while I download the photos. I email them to the group and thank them for a great day.

CROP FARMER

I grew up on a farm, so I learned a lot about farming just by helping out every day. After school, I went to agricultural college. I learned about farm technology and science, and how to manage the farm as a business, from selling crops to hiring workers. I now run my own crop farm, growing corn and soybeans. I couldn't imagine doing anything else.

As a crop farmer, I need to be an expert in lots of things: biology to understand how crops grow, math to get the right price for the crops, computers to work the machinery, and mechanics to fix it when it goes wrong!

1

During breakfast, I check the weather report for the week. If it's dry, we can harvest (gather) the crops. Wet crops clog up the machinery and stop it from working. The weather is looking good, so I call a farmhand (assistant) to meet me at the harvester—a huge machine that cuts and collects the crop.

2

The harvester is ready to go. We spend most of the day harvesting soybeans. The harvester cuts the crop and sieves out the beans, storing them in a tank. This tank is emptied into a trailer attached to a tractor that is driven by the farmhand. Driving the harvester is my favorite part of the job.

MY JOB: BEST AND WORST PARTS

BEST: Seeing the results of a great harvest is wonderful and worth all the hard work.

WORST: Big storms can ruin a whole crop—farming depends on the weather. And getting up at 5:00 a.m. every day can be tough.

3

As I'm driving, I hear a grinding noise coming from the harvester. I get out and take a look. A large tree branch has gotten caught up in the machine. I manage to pull out the branch just in time, before it causes any damage.

4

We keep harvesting till late afternoon. Now it's time to get the beans to the grain bin, where they are stored and dried. To do this, we use a machine called an auger, which is like a long tube. The trailer tips up, and then the beans move up through the auger, and pour into the grain bin.

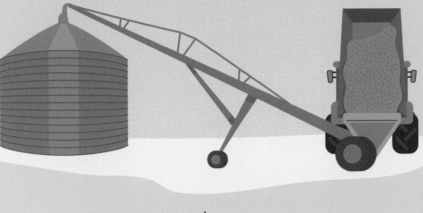

5

It's important that the beans are stored at the right temperature so they don't crack or get moldy. I place some beans inside a digital moisture tester to see how much moisture is in them. I'll do this each day, and when they're at the right moisture level and weight, I'll load them on a truck and sell them.

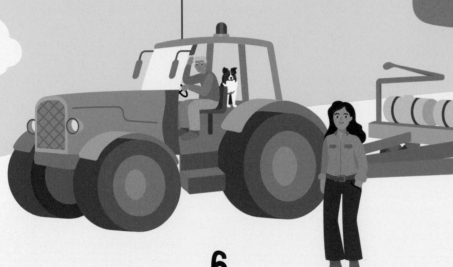

6

Next, I head back out to the fields. While we've been harvesting, another farmhand has been planting corn seeds and I want to see how he's been doing. He's been driving the planter—a machine that plants seeds in rows in the ground—and he's just finished the field when I arrive. I check that the seeds are down to the right depth (about two inches). It's looking great.

7

It's dark now, so I lock up all our machinery and head back to the farmhouse to check my emails and make some phone calls. I talk to my marketing manager, who is creating a new website for the farm. It's important for any business to have a good website, and farms are no different.

8

I finish the day by tucking into a delicious dinner made from the food grown right here on the farm.

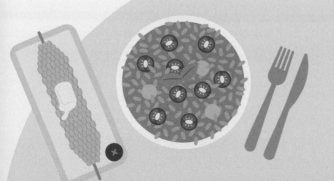

29

PARK RANGER

I've always loved nature. I grew up in the countryside, where I'd build dens or look for animals to watch and admire. I knew I wanted to work outdoors, so I earned a wildlife conservation degree in college and completed a government training program to become a park ranger.

I work for the National Park Service and spend my time helping protect and promote the park I work in. I also advise visitors on park rules and give talks to the public. No two days are the same.

1

Dawn's breaking and I'm out early on patrol. I'm looking for people who might be trying to hunt the wild animals without permission. I scan the land, but I can only see geese on the lake— and a beautiful sunrise.

2

I walk into the forest, where I come across a tree that has fallen down, blocking the path. This could be dangerous for visitors, so I report it. My coworkers will have it cleared in no time.

MY JOB: BEST AND WORST PARTS

BEST: I love encouraging visitors to enjoy the outdoors and learn about the creatures that live here.

WORST: In emergencies I might get called to work in the middle of the night.

3

I continue my checks when suddenly, I smell smoke. I notice a group of people nearby that have lit a campfire. I explain to them that fires are not allowed here, as they could cause serious damage. I put out the fire safely, and I finish my rounds without any more issues.

4

My next task is an egg hunt! We need to know which species live here in order to know how to protect them, so a big part of my job is to observe and keep records of the animals, plants, and trees in the park. Today I'm looking for birds' nests. I'll monitor any nests I find over the coming weeks and hopefully get to see some new chicks.

5

After a quick bite to eat at lunch, I head out again to check on one of the park's oldest trees. It's a 200-year-old oak tree. We've been worried because we thought the tree might be showing signs of disease. Thankfully it's looking healthy again, but I organize an appointment with an arborist (someone who plants, prunes, and keeps trees healthy) just to make sure.

6

Next, I drive over to the park's education center. I'm giving a talk to some children about the animals that live here. Encouraging others to learn how to keep wildlife safe is an important part of my job, and I love sharing my knowledge and passion.

7

The day is almost over. Visitors are leaving the park and I'm about to head home too when I receive a call from someone who has found a deer fawn curled up on the grass. I go and take a look. The fawn looks healthy—the mother deer has probably just gone for food and will be back soon. Seeing this beautiful animal is the best way to end my day.

BEACH LIFEGUARD

I grew up by the beach and I've always loved the feel of sand between my toes. I knew an office job wouldn't suit me, so I decided to turn my love of sun, sea, and surf into a career. Now I'm a beach lifeguard and I help people stay safe while they have fun.

1

I start the day by checking the weather conditions and digging flags into the sand to show people where it is safe to swim. Next, I meet with the team. At this beach, we have several lifeguards on duty at once. We take our places at the lifeguard towers and watch the water for any swimmers in trouble.

To become a lifeguard, I learned lifesaving skills, such as first aid, and took swimming and fitness tests to show that I was strong enough to rescue people from the water. I also had to learn all about the ocean and the various types of waves, tides, and currents.

3

We reach the swimmer and I have him hold on to the buoy; then I swim him to shore. I check him over—there are no signs of injury; he's just happy to be safe. The relieved people on the beach give us a cheer before I get back to my post.

2

It's a quiet morning, but just after lunch I spot someone waving their arms in panic. He has swum too far out and a strong current is pulling him out farther. I blow my whistle to let the other lifeguards know I'm about to do a rescue. I grab my rescue buoy and dive into the water, followed by another lifeguard.

MY JOB: BEST AND WORST PARTS

BEST: I get to swim in the ocean most days.

WORST: Getting stung by a jellyfish is not fun at all.

4

It's the end of the day, and there have been no more rescues. We put away our equipment and pick trash up off the beach to keep it looking its best. Then I go for a run along the beach. I need to exercise every day to keep fit.

SURF INSTRUCTOR

Surfing has been my life since I was a kid. I worked in my local surf shop whenever I could, and even made my own surfboards. As soon as I turned 16, I did first aid training and a surf instructor's course. There's a lot to learn, from equipment and lesson planning to first aid and how to keep people safe.

1

I arrive at the surf school on the beach just as the sun is rising. I chat to the other instructors and we check the reservations. I usually teach from early morning until mid-afternoon. This gives me time to go surfing myself afterward.

2

My beginner students arrive for the first lesson. We don't get in the water right away—it's easier to teach the basic moves on the beach. I show the surfers how to get on the board, how to paddle, and how to stand up and catch waves.

I teach small groups of up to eight people of all ages, from little kids to grandparents. It's never too late to start surfing.

3

Time for the ocean! We practice what I taught on the beach. As each surfer gets on the board, I give them a push. With a bit of practice, they manage to stand up for a few seconds and ride a wave.

4

In the afternoon, I eat a quick snack before teaching a group of school kids, followed by an experienced surfer who wants to improve her technique. Soon my shift is over, and then it's time to grab my board and surf till the sun sets.

MY JOB: BEST AND WORST PARTS

BEST: Seeing people surf with a big grin on their face is the best feeling.

WORST: Getting sand in my wetsuit!

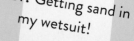

33

SEARCH & RESCUE COORDINATOR

In my job, I don't go out and rescue people—I organize rescue missions. I spent many years in the army, and when I left, I still wanted to use my outdoor skills. So, I joined a search and rescue team. Now I really enjoy making a living by helping people stay safe outdoors.

As a coordinator, I work with rescue volunteers and emergency services to help find injured or missing people in the nearby mountains. Other search and rescue coordinators work with teams who perform rescue missions at sea or in cities. You need to be a team player and be able to keep calm in this job.

1

It's early morning when I arrive at the rescue control center. From here I will receive calls and organize rescue teams when there's an emergency. It's snowing hard out there today, so who knows what the day might bring?

2

I don't have to wait long to receive my first call of the day from the police. A family out walking are trapped on a nearby mountain. One of them has hurt their leg and can't walk back in the snowy conditions. They need our help. I alert and send out a rescue team to find the family. The rescuers are skilled in first aid, using maps, and handling mountain terrain.

3

The family are stuck on a high ledge that will be tricky to find, so I call the helicopter crew to help with the search as well. After a short wait, the helicopter team call to tell me they've located the family. They confirm the GPS coordinates and I pass these on to the rescue team on the ground, so they know exactly where to find the family.

4

The rescue team, including Sammy the rescue dog, make their way to the ledge. They have radios so I can keep in touch at all times. Thankfully, they soon find the family.

5

The team tell me it's too dangerous to walk the family off the mountain, so we decide to winch each person off the ledge into the helicopter. The crew let me know once they're all safely on board.

6

The mission is a success! The injured walker will still need to be checked by a doctor, and the rest of the family will also need checking over for any injuries, so I call for an ambulance to meet them and take them to the hospital. But it's a great relief to get everyone safely off the mountain.

7

I look at the time and it's already past 1:00 p.m., so I take a break for something to eat. Then I settle down with some paperwork while I wait for any more calls. I write a report about this morning's incident. Writing reports like this is very important as it keeps track of the facts and can help us learn and improve future missions.

MY JOB: BEST AND WORST PARTS

BEST: It's a great feeling to be saving people and making them feel safe.

WORST: Sometimes, it can take a long time to rescue a stranded person; the waiting can be stressful.

8

The rest of the afternoon passes by without another call and soon it's time for me to head home. I heard that the family we rescued earlier are all home and safe now, and I'm glad today had a happy ending.

MERCHANT MARINE

Machines have always fascinated me—I loved helping my dad fix the engine of his boat, and I studied marine engineering in college. Now I work as an engineer on a huge cargo ship, looking after its machinery while it carries goods around the world.

You need good math and technology skills in this job. The ability to keep a cool head and solve problems is also very important.

1

Like always, I start the day in the engine room. Along with another engineer, I'm inspecting the machinery to look for any leaks or problems. My senses often help me—a bad smell, a strange sound, or an oil leak are all signs that something needs to be fixed.

2

After the inspection, it's my turn to be on watch in the control room. I'll be here for about four hours. I have to stay alert—if something goes wrong it's up to me to report it and begin repairing it.

3

My next task is to help with refueling the ship. We need fuel to keep the ship's engines running, so we pull into port and attach a hose from a fuel barge to our ship. It takes about nine hours to refuel a ship like ours, so I take my break and explore the town. I love trying the local food wherever we go.

MY JOB: BEST AND WORST PARTS

BEST: I get to use all my engineering skills and travel around the world at the same time.

WORST: I'm often sailing for months at a time, so I do miss my family and friends.

4

Back on the ship, I spend the afternoon making a list of any parts or tools we need to restock. Soon the day is over and it's time to relax. I hang out with some of the crew before I head to my cabin to sleep.

SAILING INSTRUCTOR

I started learning to sail at my local sailing club when I was eight. With lots of practice and training, my confidence grew and I was soon taking part in races. I started volunteering when I was 16, and then took courses to become an instructor. Teaching sailing is really fun.

1

Today, I'm teaching a group of children how to sail. Each child is fitted with a life jacket. I make sure they wear a hat too, to protect them from the strong sun.

2

I give each child a small boat with a sail. After teaching them the parts of the boat and how to sail safely, we attach the sail to each boat and work together to carry the boats to the water.

As an instructor, it's important to be fit and to be a good swimmer—and sailor, of course. I teach people of all ages to sail all kinds of boats, from small dinghies to large yachts.

3

I'm sailing in my own boat close to my class. The kids practice using the tiller (the lever used for steering left and right), and tightening and loosening the rope to manage the sail. They're doing really well.

4

After a break for lunch, we stay out of the water to learn how to take the sail off the boat and store it. Everyone has worked really hard and had loads of fun. I finish the day by rewarding the kids with their very own sailor badge.

MY JOB: BEST AND WORST PARTS

BEST: Seeing my students sail with confidence and having fun.

WORST: The wind! Too much or too little means no sailing.

37

CIVIL ENGINEER

I design and help build all kinds of structures we see around us, from roads and bridges to parks and train stations. I was always interested in math and design at school, so I decided to study civil engineering in college. Today, I'm a civil engineer for an engineering services company.

There's lots of variety in my job. I spend some of my time working in an office, designing plans, and making calculations for new builds. I spend the rest of my time outdoors, checking new building sites and projects.

1

I start the day in the office. I'm working on a project to build a new bridge over a highway, so I meet with my team of designers and architects. They will work out the outside appearance and design of the bridge. I take a look at their designs so far. It's looking great.

2

My job is to work out how to build the bridge, if it will be safe, and what materials we need to use. I use special computer programs to run tests on the architects' plans to make sure the bridge will stay up during high winds and storms.

3

Next, I leave the office to meet the construction manager who is managing another building project we're working on: a new bridge over a river. I've come to inspect the site to check the quality of the work. So far, so good.

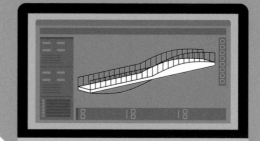

4

I grab a quick lunch and then I visit a site nearby where we are planning to build a new park. I meet with an official from the local government. He wants to see if the site will be a suitable place to build the park. I hope he will give us permission, as it will be a great addition to the city.

5

After the meeting, I head back to the office and make some rough plans for the park. Part of my job is to work out how much all the materials will cost and make sure we don't spend too much.

6

My last job of the day is to inspect a section of the city's railroad track. As well as building new structures, I take care of the old ones, too—checking for any signs of damage. I notice a few issues, so I make sure this part of the track is closed until it's repaired. Keeping people safe is the most important part of my job.

TYPES OF CIVIL ENGINEERING

There are five main areas of civil engineering and the work is different in each one. These are: structural (structures such as bridges), transportation (the flow of people and goods from one place to another), environmental (for example, water treatment and waste management), geotechnical (anything beneath the ground, such as foundations), and coastal (anything to do with the shoreline, such as building artificial harbors).

MY JOB: BEST AND WORST PARTS

BEST: Building a new bridge or building that will be used by people for a long time is a great feeling.

WORST: If I make a mistake in my work, it can cost a lot of money as a project might have to be rebuilt.

7

Soon my working day is over, but the engineering doesn't stop there! I spend my evening listening to music and working on one of my model building sets—this one is a model plane.

BOTANIST

Botanists are scientists who study plant life. My love of plants started in my family garden, where I collected all kinds of leaves and flowers. My fascination is never ending, and today I'm a college professor of botany. I teach, do research, and travel the world, searching for new and interesting plants—it's my dream job!

There are many kinds of botanists. Some, like me, collect new plant species, in order to learn more about them. Others are interested in finding plants to make medicine or studying how plants are affected by pollution.

1

It's early morning and my research assistant and I are on a research trip. My work can take me all over the world, to tropical forests or snowy woodlands, but today I'm only traveling a few miles from the college. We're visiting a small uninhabited island nearby, to collect plants and make a list of what grows there.

2

Once we're on land, we collect the plants by taking small pieces, called cuttings. I carefully lay them on a sheet of paper in the plant press. This will press the plants and dry them out, protecting them from damage. We also write labels to identify the plants and where we found them.

MY JOB: BEST AND WORST PARTS

BEST: My job gives me the chance to protect our natural world and help people understand why that's important.

WORST: It can be very physically demanding. Hiking up mountains or working in hot rain forests to collect samples is hard work.

3

We place any plant parts that can't be pressed, such as berries or pieces of bark, in a botanist's bag, called a vasculum. We work hard through the morning—it's hot and tiring, and there are tons of bugs—but I don't mind. I love being surrounded by all these fascinating plants.

4

After lunch, I find some strange-looking berries that I've never seen before—I will examine them more closely back at the lab. Who knows what special properties they might have? Some plants are pretty powerful and can help us treat diseases.

5

Around mid-afternoon, after we've collected as many specimens as we can, we return to the college. We take our findings to the herbarium, where we store all the plants we find. Many colleges have herbariums, and scientists from around the world visit them. We're always excited to share all the interesting new specimens we've collected.

6

Next, I head back to my office where I spend some time writing a report about today's findings. Writing reports like this is a big part of my job; I have to write reports before, during, and after all research trips.

7

My last task of the day is to prepare a presentation. I'm teaching tomorrow and I'll be sharing my team's research. Teaching is a very important part of my job, and I always make sure to prepare and practice beforehand. I love passing on my knowledge.

8

Soon my day comes to an end and I make my way home. I can't wait for dinner—can you guess what's on the menu? It's roasted vegetables and fruit salad tonight—I just can't get enough of plants!

LAND SURVEYOR

I always knew I wanted to work outdoors. I also really enjoy math—especially measuring things! So, after my geography degree, I did further training to become a surveyor while working as an assistant. I now work for a large company where I measure land, gather data, and create maps for building projects. A talent for numbers and technology is key in my job.

1

This morning I'm visiting a site with an assistant surveyor. We're here to measure the site's boundaries (the lines on a map that divide one property from another) and form a detailed picture of the size, shape, and features of the land. The ground is quite rough, so we travel on all-terrain vehicles. It's a fun way to get to work!

2

Once we're on site, we set up our global positioning system (GPS) equipment. These instruments connect with satellites in space to give us precise locations and measurements. We gather and record information for the whole site. Later we will use this data to create a map of the area.

I work with a variety of different people, such as construction site managers (see pages 20–21), civil engineers (see pages 38–39), and cartographers (see page 47). That's what makes it so interesting!

4

Soon it's time for home. Before I leave, I have a quick look at what's in store for tomorrow—I'll be surveying a site for a new sports stadium project. No two days are ever the same in this job!

MY JOB: BEST AND WORST PARTS

BEST: I love working with the latest technologies, such as GPS systems and drones.

WORST: Sometimes I find myself in uncomfortable places, such as steep cliffs or muddy ditches.

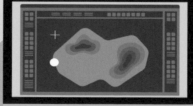
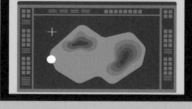

3

We finish our survey and break for lunch before we head back to the office. I download the data we collected and spend the rest of the day using a computer program to draw a map of the site. When it's finished, I'll pass the map on to the construction company that hired us to carry out the survey.

LINE WORKER

When I was younger, I used to watch line workers at work. It looked so exciting it made me want to do their job. I help to keep power flowing to people's homes. Working outside, I install and repair overhead electrical power lines, and deal with emergencies, such as power cuts. In this job, it's important to be fit, strong, and have a good head for heights!

After high school, I became an apprentice with a local power company. I learned how to climb safely and operate the equipment. Although it can be dangerous work, we receive training to keep us safe.

1

It's 3:30 a.m. when I wake up to the sound of my phone ringing. I'm on call, which means it's my turn to deal with any emergencies. I'm told that there's been a snowstorm and part of the town is without power.

2

I meet the other on-call line workers at the first emergency: a tree branch has fallen on a power line. We check that the main power is off for this section. It's dangerous to work around live electric cables, and safety always comes first. Then, I remove the branch using a bucket lift to reach it.

MY JOB: BEST AND WORST PARTS

BEST: Climbing so high means there are great views—I can see for miles around.

WORST: Sometimes I miss out on important family events—when the power goes out, I have to work.

3

The work's not over—there's an issue with one of the poles. I need to replace a damaged part, called the fuse. This pole is in an awkward place—the truck and lift can't get to it, so I climb up and replace the part. It's windy up here, but my harness keeps me safe.

4

At last, the power's on! It's morning now, so we go to a cafe for a well-earned breakfast before I head home to catch up on some sleep.

YOUR PERFECT JOB MATCH

With so many jobs out there, it can be tricky to choose between them. Use this guide to find out which careers match up with your skills, personal qualities, and interests.

Botanist

Geologist

Paleontologist

Ecologist

Good at science

Marine biologist

These jobs are perfect if you love learning and investigating.

To work in these careers, it helps if you enjoy being part of a group.

Landscape gardener

Wildland firefighter

Team player

Beach lifeguard

Forester   Search & rescue coordinator

Organized

Construction site manager

WHAT ARE YOUR SKILLS?

If you are good at planning and paying attention to detail, these jobs could be ideal for you.

Plant nursery manager

Adventure guide

Great with people

Listening to and understanding other people are key skills in these jobs.

Campsite manager

Crop farmer

Civil engineer

Good with technology

Merchant marine

Land surveyor

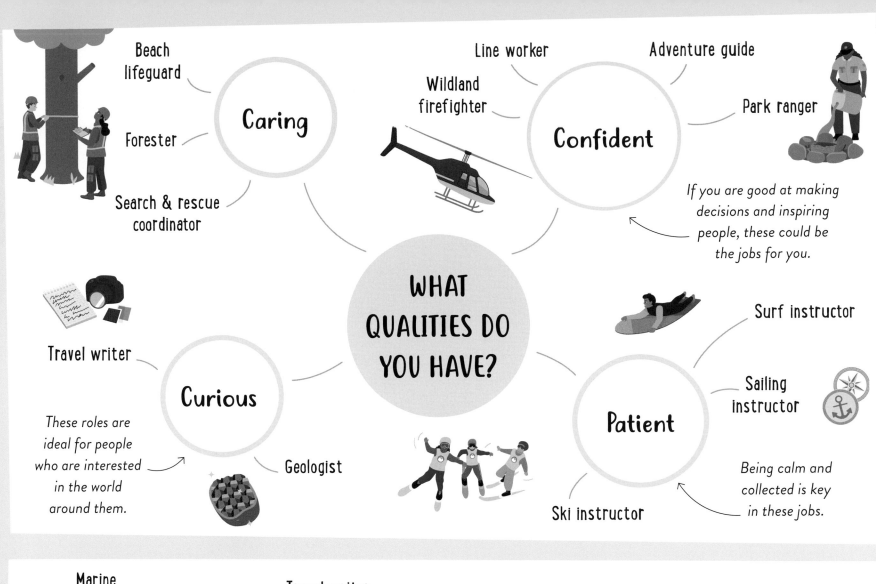

Caring

Beach lifeguard

Forester

Search & rescue coordinator

Confident

Line worker

Wildland firefighter

Adventure guide

Park ranger

If you are good at making decisions and inspiring people, these could be the jobs for you.

WHAT QUALITIES DO YOU HAVE?

Curious

Travel writer

Geologist

These roles are ideal for people who are interested in the world around them.

Patient

Surf instructor

Sailing instructor

Ski instructor

Being calm and collected is key in these jobs.

Travel

Marine biologist

Travel writer

Merchant marine

Paleontologist

Are you looking for adventure? These jobs often involve exploring the world's oceans, deserts, and sights.

WHAT ARE YOUR INTERESTS AND GOALS?

Protecting nature

Many jobs that involve working outdoors are all about caring for and protecting wildlife.

Botanist

Ecologist

Park ranger

Wildlife officer

Keeping active

Landscape gardener

Surf instructor

Ski instructor

If keeping fit is important to you, then these jobs could be just right.

45

THERE'S MORE ...

You've read about a lot of careers working in the outdoors in this book, but there are even more to choose from. Some of these were mentioned very briefly in the book and others will be completely new to you.

TRAVEL PHOTOGRAPHER

For those with a passion for photography and travel, this could be the perfect job! Travel photographers might be hired by companies such as magazine publishers to visit places and take photos for them. As well as being skilled at taking pictures, travel photographers need to be happy with traveling alone, sleeping in strange places, and very long journeys!

TREE SURGEON

Tree surgeons take care of trees. They plant them, help to keep them healthy, and sometimes have to cut them down. To do this job, it's important to be strong and fit and, of course, have a good head for heights! It can also be dangerous, since it involves a lot of climbing and using powerful equipment, so getting proper training is essential.

COMMERCIAL FISHER

Commercial fishers work on ships, catching fish for people to eat. They use nets and traps to catch the fish, and they need to enjoy working hard, as the days can be long and tiring. It also helps to be good at getting along with other people, as fishers often spend weeks together out at sea.

CARTOGRAPHER

For anyone who enjoys looking at maps and wonders how they are made, a cartography career could be just for them! Cartographers create maps. They spend time outdoors gathering information about the landscape. They then use computer programs to design and produce the maps. Creativity and a good eye for detail are useful skills in this job.

METEOROLOGIST

Meteorologists are weather scientists. They study the atmosphere (the air around our planet) and predict how it will affect our weather. Some meteorologists work as weather forecasters. They use special computers to predict our weather and produce reports for TV or radio. Others work as researchers, investigating our weather in more detail, from climate change to flooding.

ARCHEOLOGIST

These scientists study objects from the past to help them learn about how humans lived long ago. Archeologists work all over the world at outdoor sites known as digs. Using special tools, they dig up objects buried in the ground, then study and write reports about them. Anyone who loves history and science— and doesn't mind getting a bit muddy—will enjoy this job!

P.E. TEACHER

P.E. teachers need a love of sports and plenty of energy! They must be familiar with lots of different sports, from basketball to gymnastics, and know about the human body, including how to treat injuries. Being organized helps, too, since they have to prepare lessons for their students, and arrange sporting events and trips.

First American Edition 2020
Kane Miller, A Division of EDC Publishing

Copyright © 2020 Quarto Publishing plc

For information contact:
Kane Miller, A Division of EDC Publishing
PO Box 470663
Tulsa, OK 74147-0663
www.kanemiller.com
www.edcpub.com
www.usbornebooksandmore.com

Library of Congress Control Number: 2020930650

Manufactured in Guangdong, China CC072020

ISBN: 978-1-68464-089-8

1 2 3 4 5 6 7 8 9 10

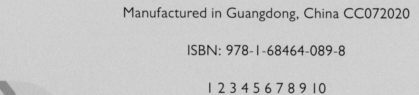

MIX
Paper from
responsible sources
FSC
www.fsc.org
FSC® C008047